VOL. 15

HAL•LEONARD GUITAR PLAY-ALONG

AUDIO ACCESS INCLUDED

R&B

T0040837

Tracking, mixing, and mastering by Jake Johnson
All guitars by Doug Boduch
Bass by Tom McGirr
Keyboards by Warren Wiegratz
Drums by Scott Schroèdl

PLAYBACK+
Speed • Pitch • Balance • Loop

To access audio visit:
www.halleonard.com/mylibrary

Enter Code
4569-5376-6048-8033

ISBN 978-0-634-05635-2

Visit Hal Leonard Online at
www.halleonard.com

Contact us:
Hal Leonard
7777 West Bluemound Road
Milwaukee, WI 53213
Email: info@halleonard.com

In Europe, contact:
Hal Leonard Europe Limited
42 Wigmore Street
Marylebone, London, W1U 2RN
Email: info@halleonardeurope.com

In Australia, contact:
Hal Leonard Australia Pty. Ltd.
4 Lentara Court
Cheltenham, Victoria, 3192 Australia
Email: info@halleonard.com.au

CONTENTS

Ain't Too Proud to Beg

Words and Music by Edward Holland and Norman Whitfield

𝄋 **Verse**

Moderately ♩ = 126

2nd, 3rd, & 4th times, substitute Fill 1

1. I know you wan-na leave me, but I re-fuse to let you go.
2., 3., 4. *See additional lyrics*

mf
w/ clean tone

If I have to beg, plead for your sym-pa-thy, I don't mind 'cause you mean that

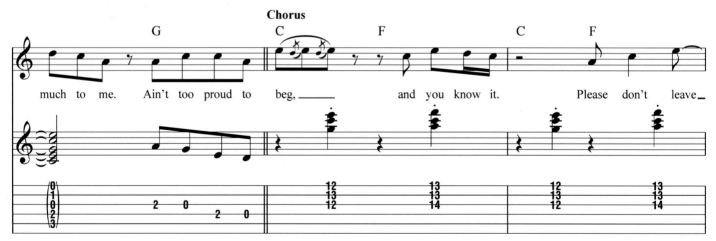

much to me. Ain't too proud to beg, and you know it. Please don't leave

Chorus

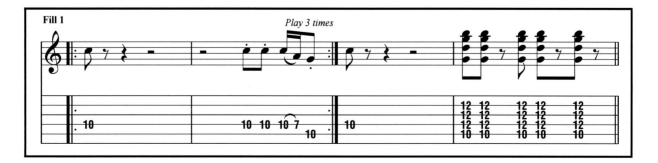

Fill 1

Play 3 times

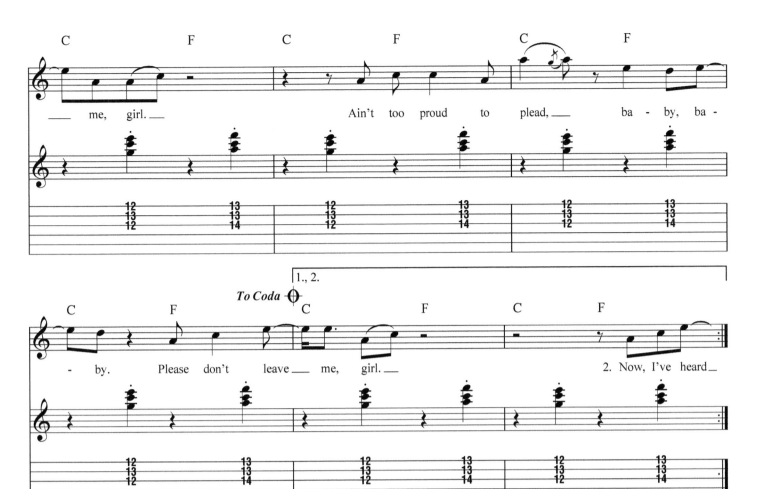

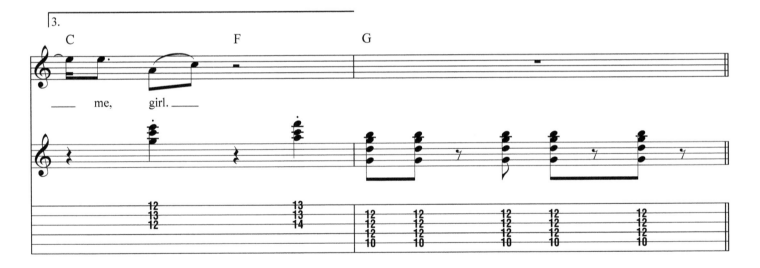

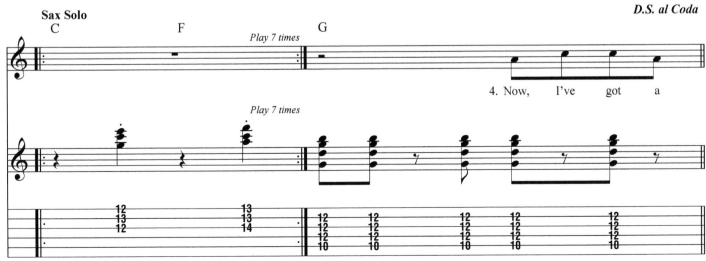

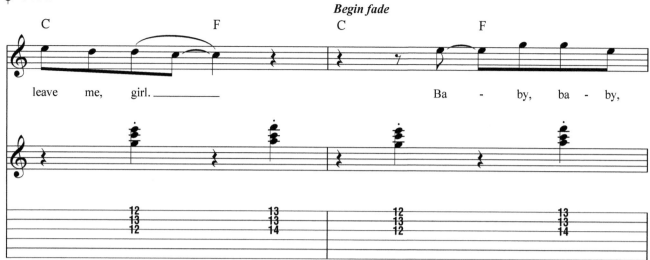

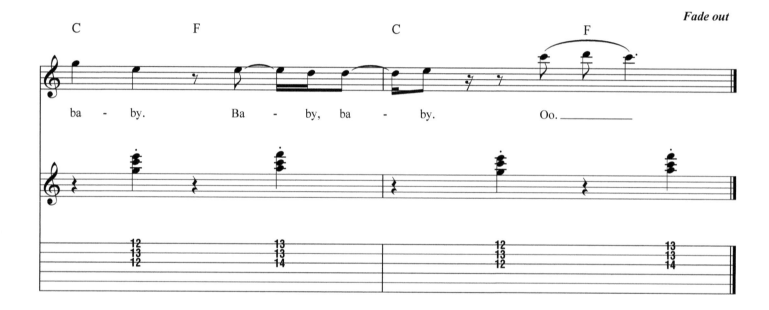

Additional Lyrics

2. Now, I've heard a cryin' man is half a man,
   With no sense of pride.
   But if I have to cry to keep you, I don't mind weepin'
   If it'll keep you by my side.

3. If I have to sleep on your doorstep all night and day
   Just to keep you from walking away.
   Let your friends laugh, even this I can stand,
   'Cause I wanna keep you any way I can.

4. Now, I've got a love so deep in the pit of my heart,
   And each day it grows more and more.
   I'm not ashamed to call and plead to you, baby,
   If pleading keeps you from walking out that door.

Brick House

Words and Music by Lionel Richie, Ronald LaPread, Walter Orange, Milan Williams, Thomas McClary and William King

Intro
Moderately ♩ = 102

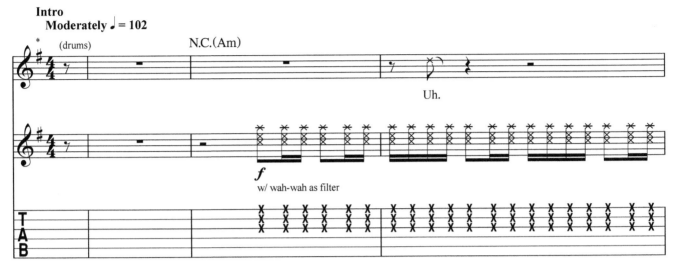

*Key signature denotes A Dorian.

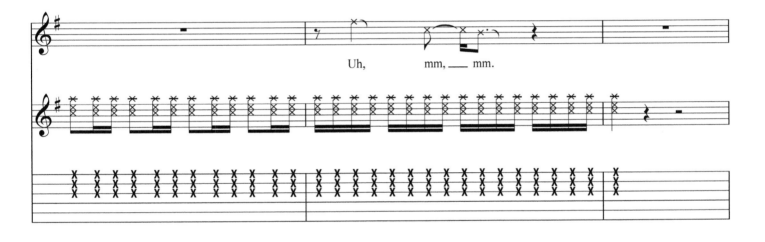

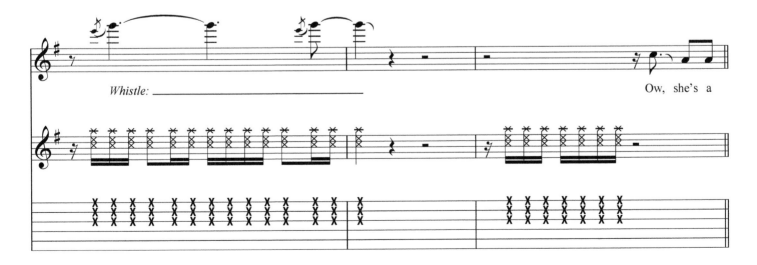

Chorus

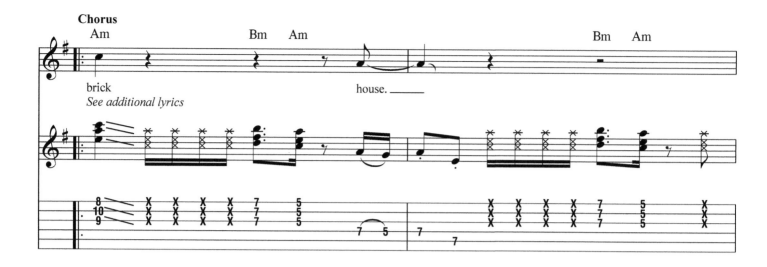

brick   house.

See additional lyrics

She's might-y, might-y ____ just let-tin' it all ___ hang out. ___ Ah, she's a

brick   house. ___   I like la-dies stacked ___ and that's a fact. ___

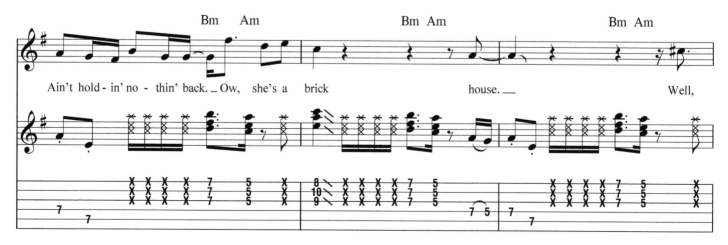

Ain't hold-in' no-thin' back. ___ Ow, she's a brick   house. ___   Well,

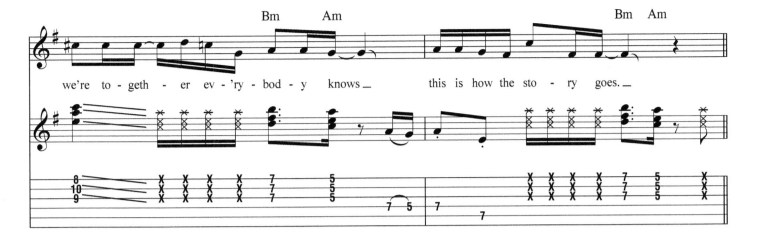

we're to-geth-er ev-'ry-bod-y knows __ this is how the sto-ry goes. __

Verse

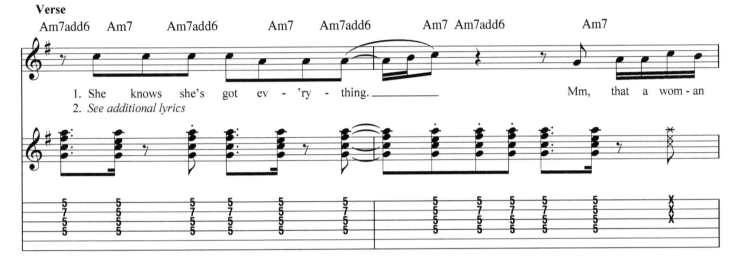

Am7add6 Am7 Am7add6 Am7 Am7add6 Am7 Am7add6 Am7

1. She knows she's got ev-'ry-thing. _____ Mm, that a wom-an
2. *See additional lyrics*

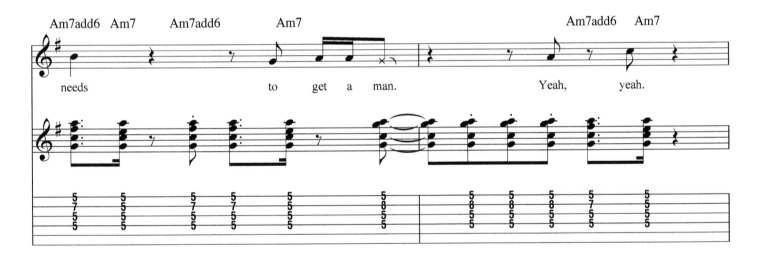

Am7add6 Am7 Am7add6 Am7 Am7add6 Am7

needs to get a man. Yeah, yeah.

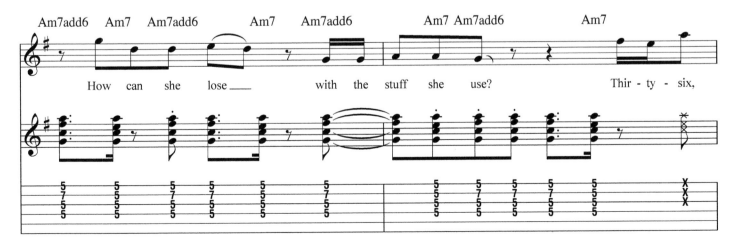

Am7add6 Am7 Am7add6 Am7 Am7add6 Am7 Am7add6 Am7

How can she lose __ with the stuff she use? Thir-ty-six,

twen-ty-four,____ thir-ty-six. Ow, what a win-ning hand-ful. She's a

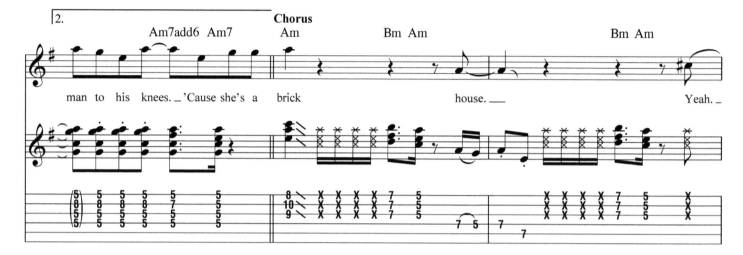

man to his knees. _'Cause she's a brick house. ____ Yeah. _

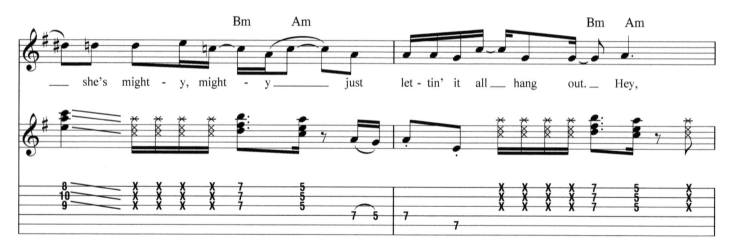

____ she's might-y, might-y_____ just let-tin' it all _ hang out. _ Hey,

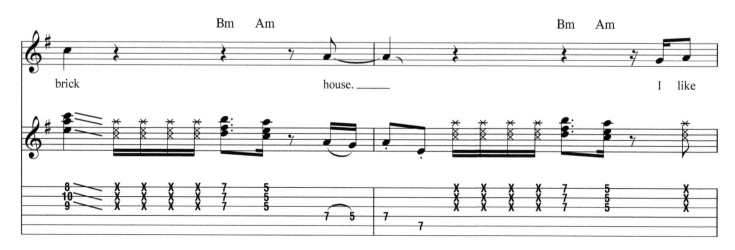

brick house. ____ I like

Yeah, she's might-y, might-y _____ a just

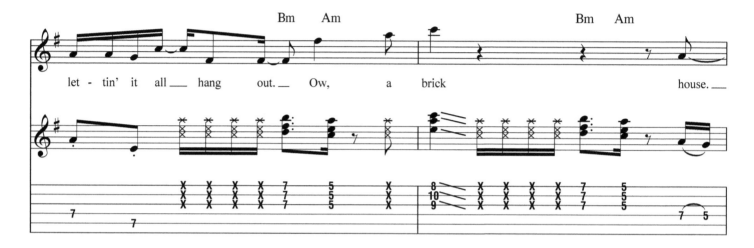

let-tin' it all __ hang out.__ Ow, a brick house.__

Yeah, she's the one,__ the on-ly one__

Bridge

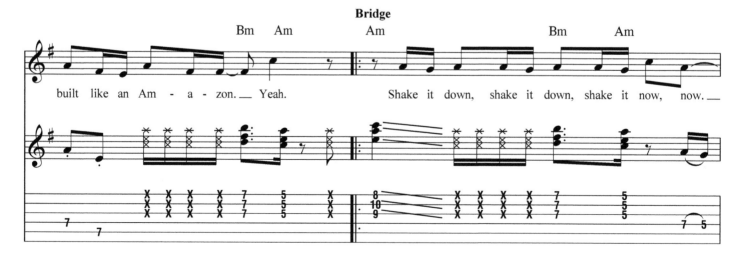

built like an Am-a-zon.__ Yeah. Shake it down, shake it down, shake it now, now.__

Additional Lyrics

Chorus She's a brick house.
She's mighty, mighty, just lettin' it all hang out.
Ah, she's a brick house.
Oh, I like ladies stacked and that's a fact.
Ain't holdin' nothin' back.
Oh, she's a brick house.
Yeah, she's the one, the only one
Built like an Amazon.

2. Mm, the clothes she wear, her sexy ways
Make an old man wish for younger days, yeah, yeah.
She knows she's built and knows how to please.
Sure 'nough can knock a strong man to his knees.

Get Ready

Words and Music by William "Smokey" Robinson

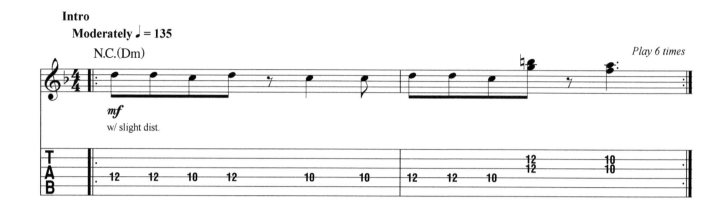

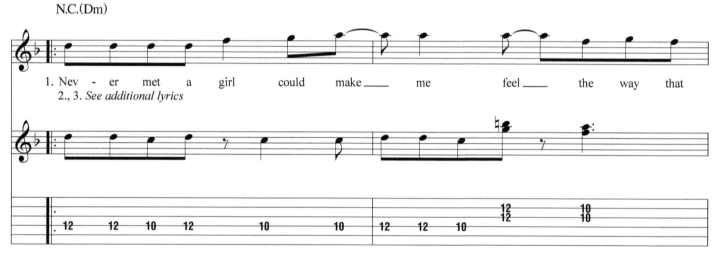

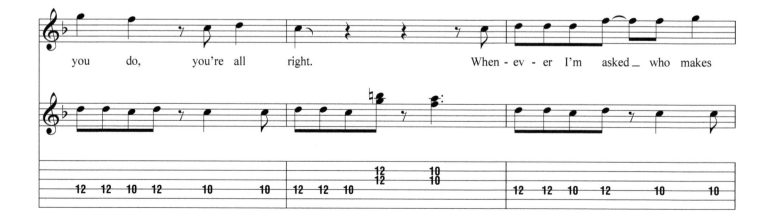

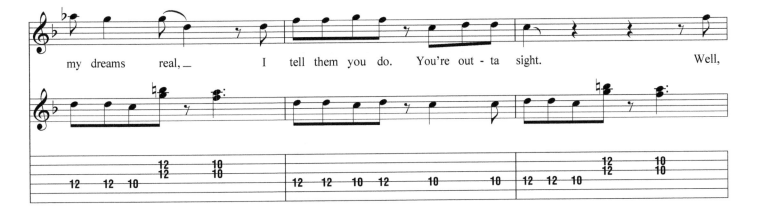

my dreams real, __ I tell them you do. You're out - ta sight. Well,

twee - dle - e - dee, __ twee - dle - e - dum. __ Look out, ba - by, 'cause

Chorus
F

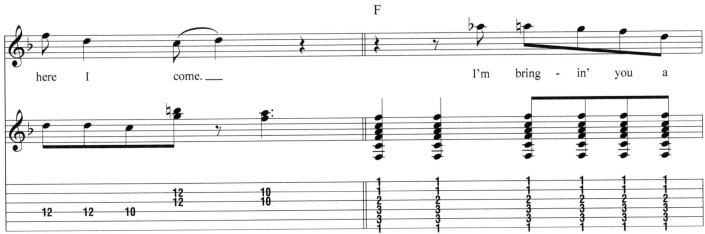

here I come. __ I'm bring - in' you a

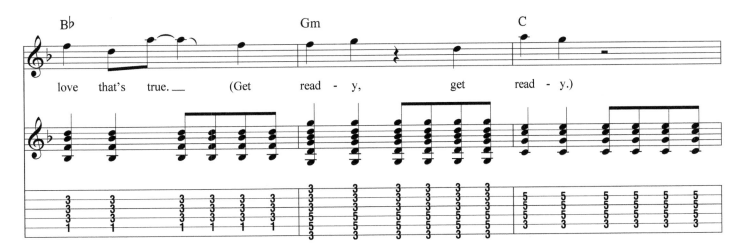

love that's true. __ (Get read - y, get read - y.)

I'll start mak-in' love to you. Get read - y, get

read - y. (Get read - y, 'cause here I come. _

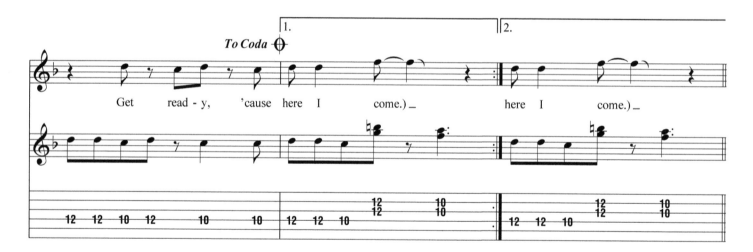

Get read - y, 'cause here I come.) _ here I come.) _

Saxophone Solo

D.S. al Coda

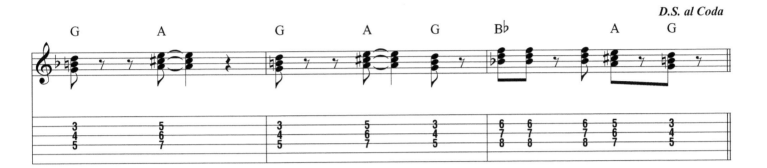

$\oint$ **Coda**

Outro

w/ Voc. ad lib., till fade

N.C.(Dm)

Repeat and fade

here I come.)_ (Get read-y, 'cause here I come.)_

Additional Lyrics

2. You wanna play hide and seek with love,
   Let me remind ya,
   Lovin', you're gonna miss
   And the time it takes to find ya.
   Well, fee, fi, fo, fum.
   Look out, baby, now, here I come.

3. If all my friends should want me to,
   I think I'll understand.
   Hope I get to you before they do,
   'Cause that's how I planned it.
   Well, tweedle-e-dee, now, tweedle-e-dum.
   Look out, baby, now, here I come.

I Can't Help Myself
(Sugar Pie, Honey Bunch)

Words and Music by Brian Holland, Lamont Dozier and Edward Holland

I can't help my - self.   I love ___ you and

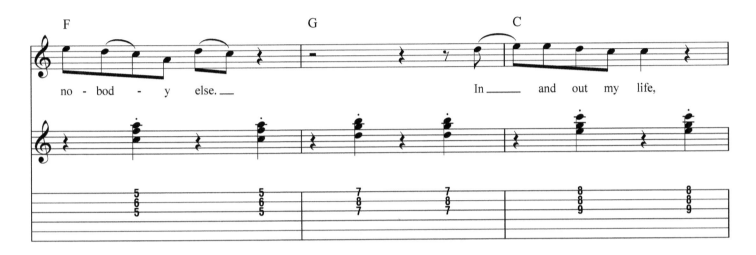

no - bod - y else. ___   In ___ and out my life,

you come and you go ___   leav - ing ___ just ___ your

pic - ture be - hind. ___   And I kissed it a thou - sand times. ___   2. When ___

Verse

you snap your fin - ger or wink your eyes, __ I come a run - nin' to you. __

5. See additional lyrics

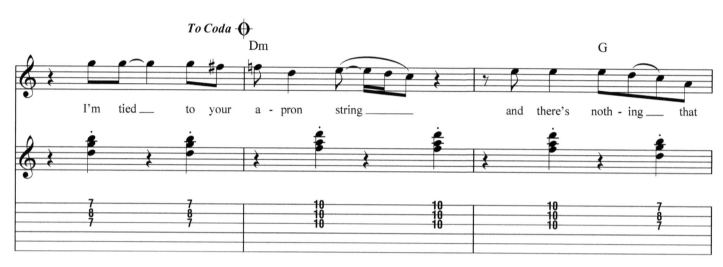

To Coda

I'm tied __ to your a - pron string __ and there's noth - ing __ that

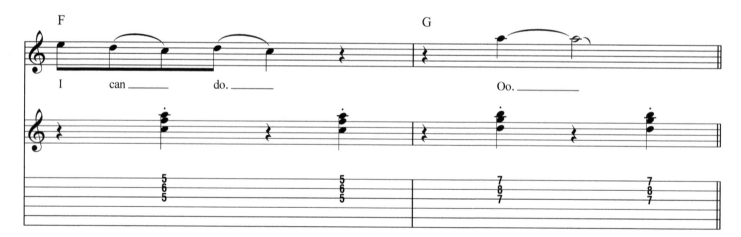

I can __ do. __ Oo. __

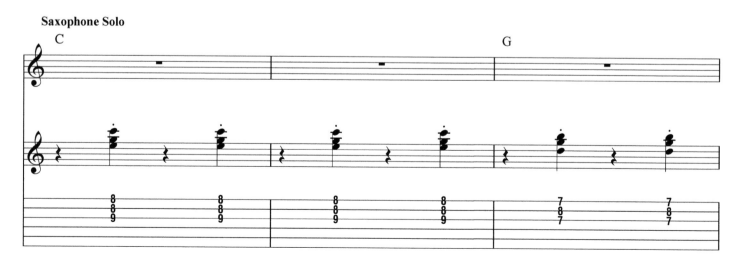

Saxophone Solo

Can't help my - self, _____ no, _____ I _____ can't _____

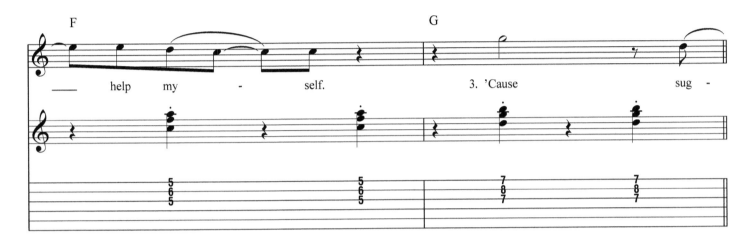

_____ help my - self. 3. 'Cause _____ sug -

Verse

- ar pie, hon - ey bunch, I'm weak - er than a man should be. _____

I can't help my - self. _____ I'm a fool _____ in _____

love, __ you see. __ Wan - na tell __ you I don't love you, tell __

__ you that we're through. And I've tried, __ but ev - 'ry time __ I

see your face __ I get all __ choked up in - side. __ When __

Interlude

__ I call your name, girl, __ it starts to flame. (Burn - in' in my heart, tear'n' __

⊕ Coda

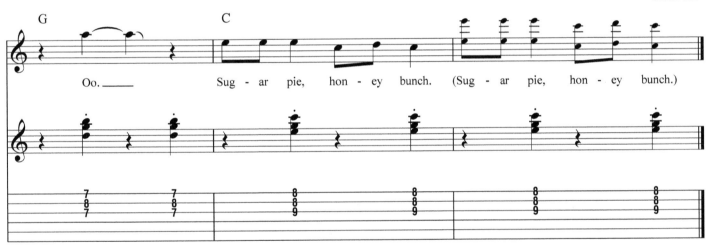

Additional Lyrics

4. 'Cause sugar pie, honey bunch,
   You know that I'm waitin' for you.
   Can't help myself.
   I love you and nobody else.
   In and out my life,
   You come and you go
   Leaving just your picture behind.
   And I kissed it a thousand times.

5. Sugar pie, honey bunch,
   You know that I love you.
   Can't help myself,
   No, I can't help myself. Oo.
   Sugar pie, honey bunch. (Sugar pie, honey bunch.)

I Got You
(I Feel Good)

Words and Music by James Brown

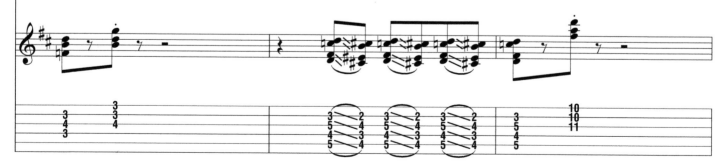

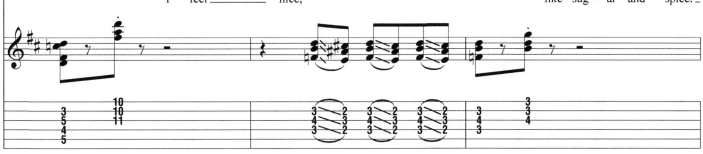

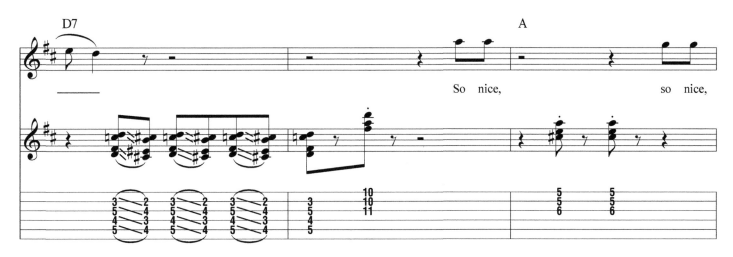

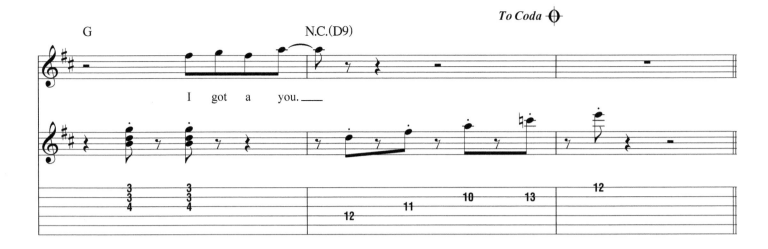

I got a you.___

Interlude

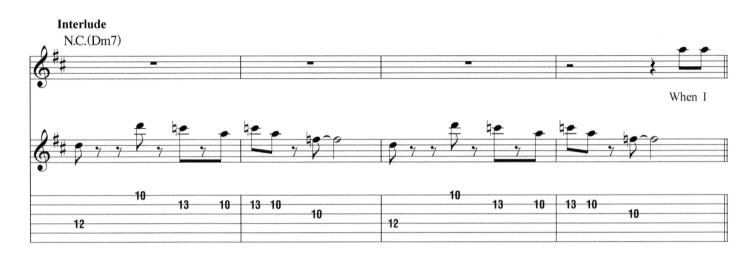

When I

Bridge

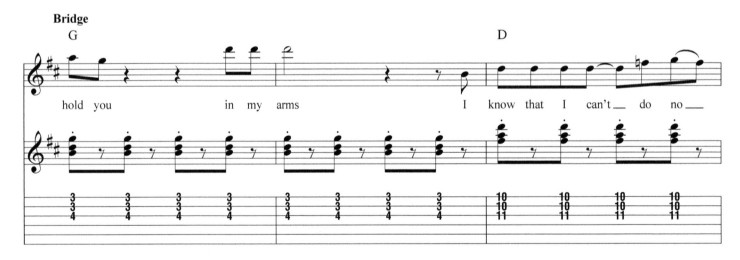

hold you in my arms I know that I can't__ do no___

wrong.___ And__ when I hold_____ you in_____ my arms my

Additional Lyrics

4. And I feel nice,
   Like sugar and spice.
   I feel nice,
   Like sugar and spice.
   So nice, so nice
   That I got a you.

5. Wow! I feel good,
   I knew that I would, now.
   I feel good,
   I knew that I would.
   So good, so good
   That I got a you.

I Heard It Through the Grapevine

Words and Music by Norman J. Whitfield and Barrett Strong

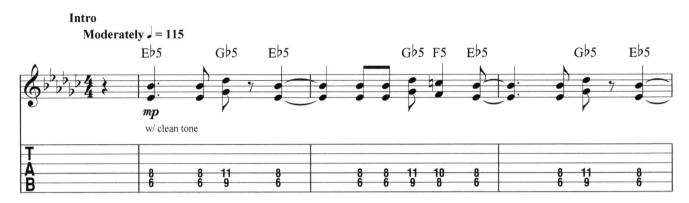

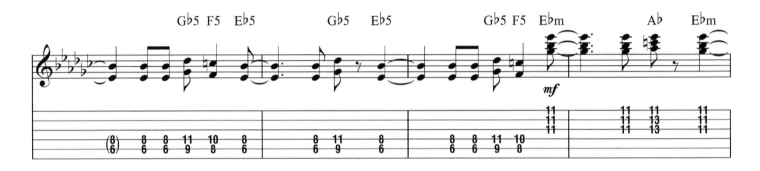

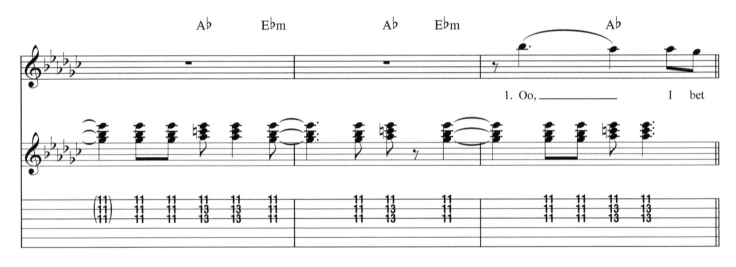

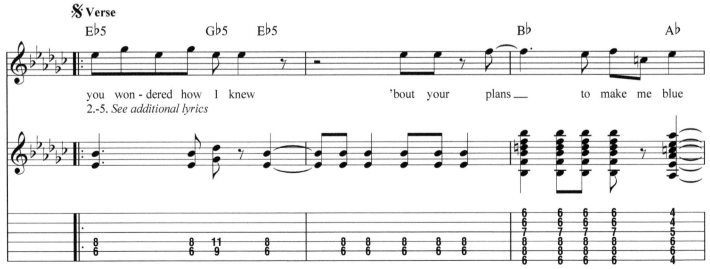

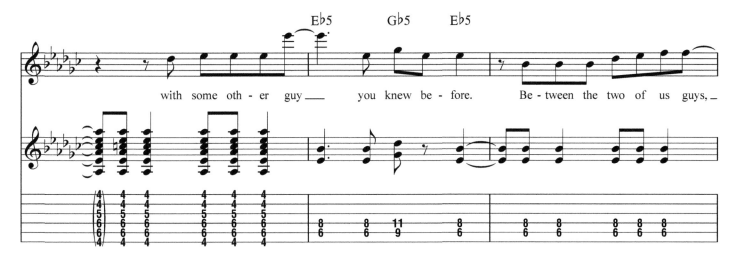

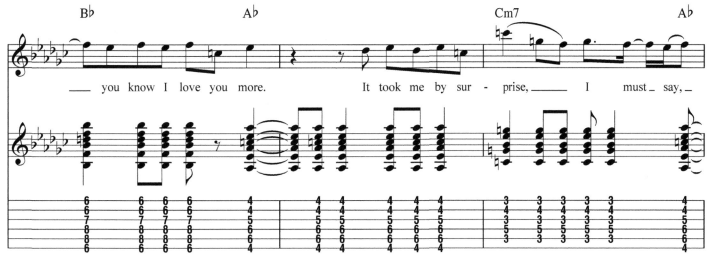

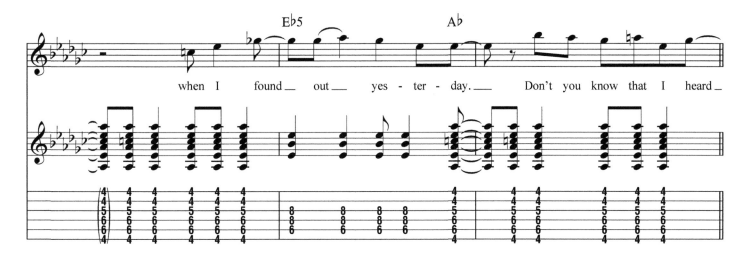

Chorus

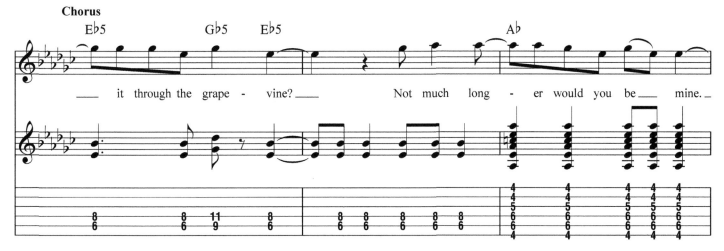

Interlude

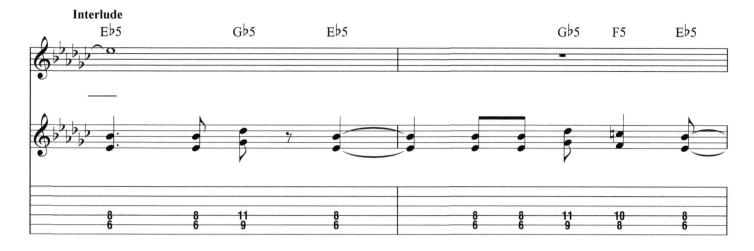

1st time, D.S.
(take repeat)
2nd time, D.S. al Coda

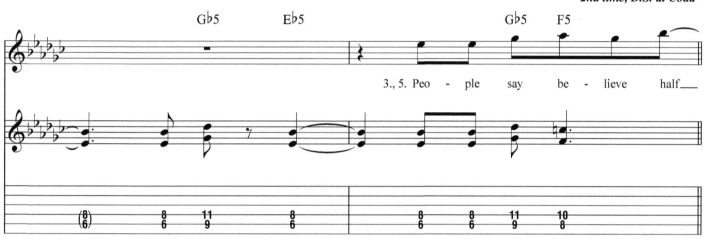

3., 5. Peo - ple say be - lieve half___

⊕ Coda

Outro
Repeat and fade

w/ Voc. ad lib., till fade

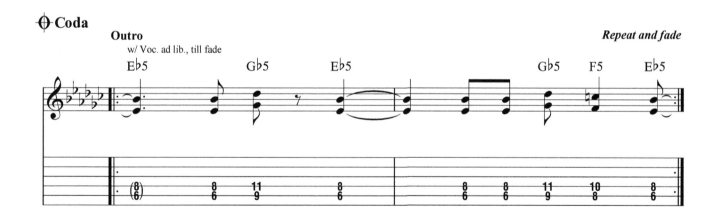

Additional Lyrics

2., 4. I know a man ain't supposed to cry,
But these tears, I can't hold inside.
Losing you would end my life, you see.
'Cause you mean that much to me.
You could've told me yourself that you love someone else.
Instead, I heard...

3., 5. People say believe half of what you see.
Some and none of what you hear.
But I can't help from being confused.
If it's true, please tell me dear.
Do you plan to let me go for the other guy you loved before?

My Girl

Words and Music by William "Smokey" Robinson and Ronald White

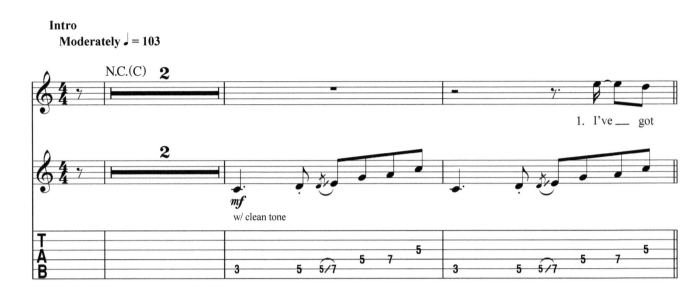

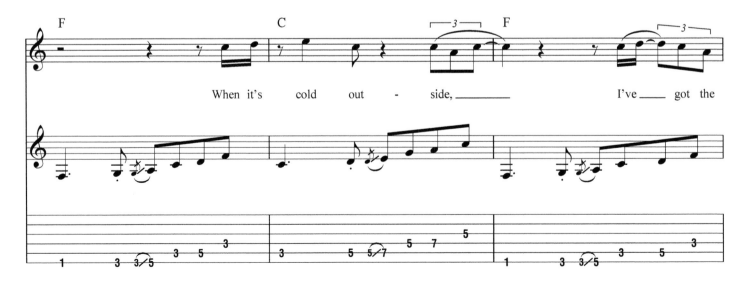

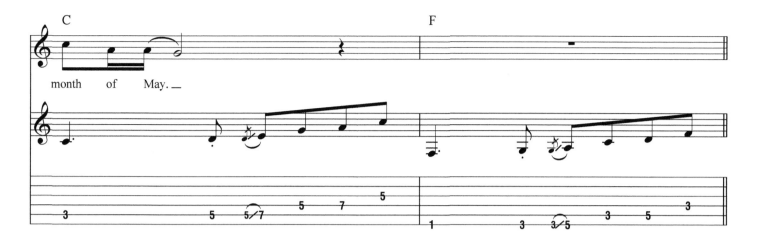

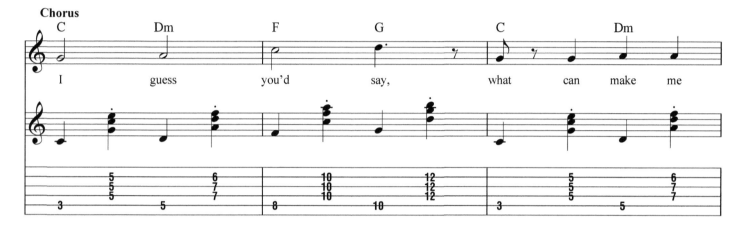

Chorus

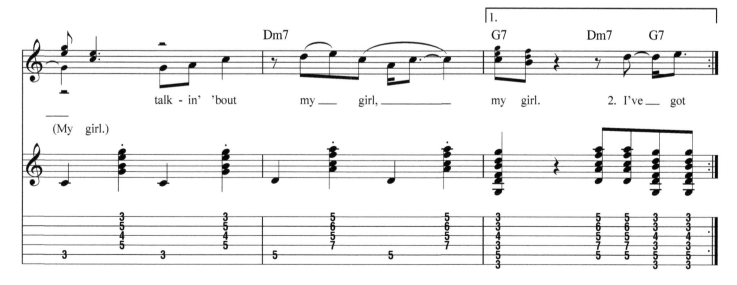

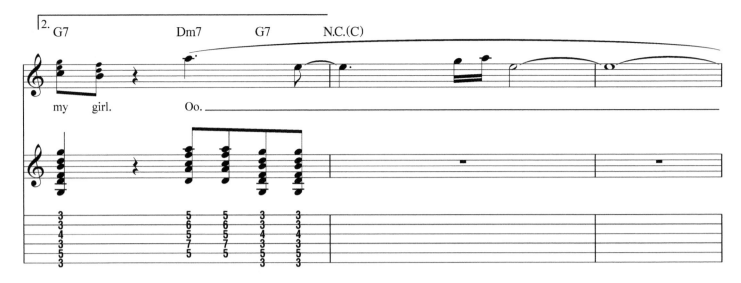

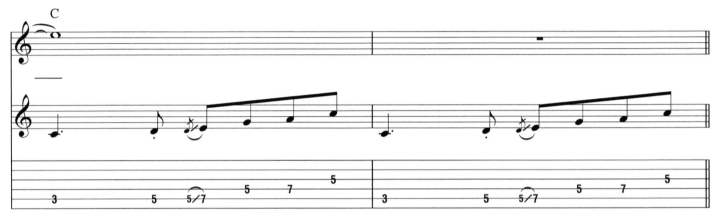

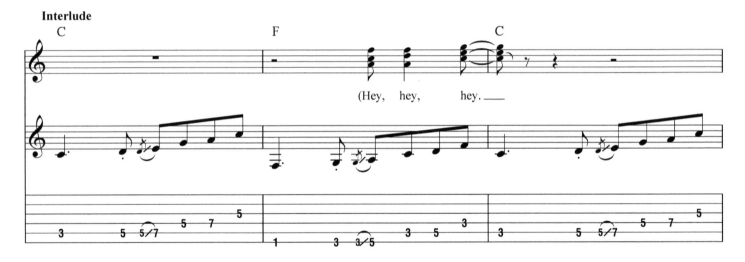

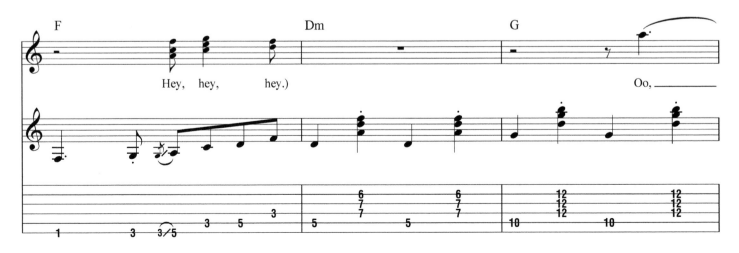

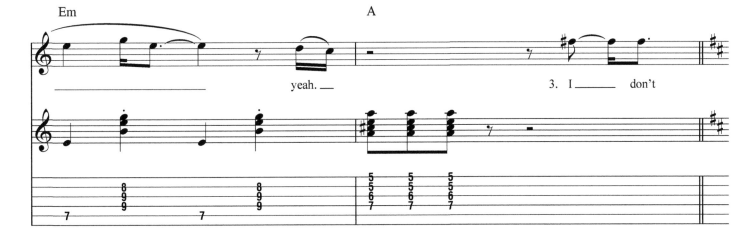

yeah. ___ 3. I ___ don't

Verse

need no ___ mon - ey, ___ for - tune,

or fame. _____ I got

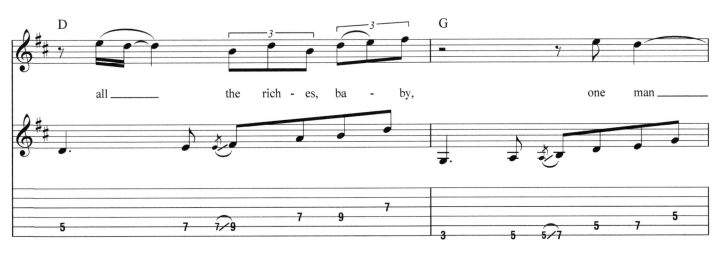

all ___ the rich - es, ba - by, one man ___

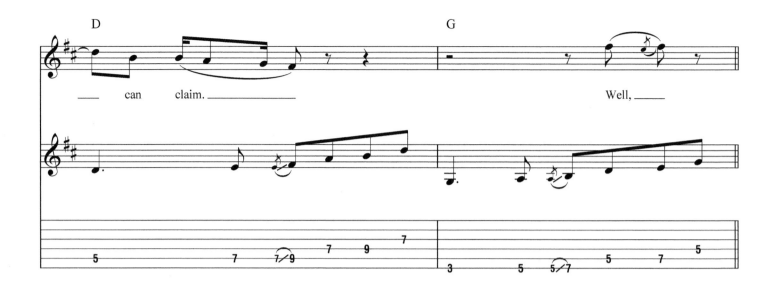

can claim. _____ Well, _____

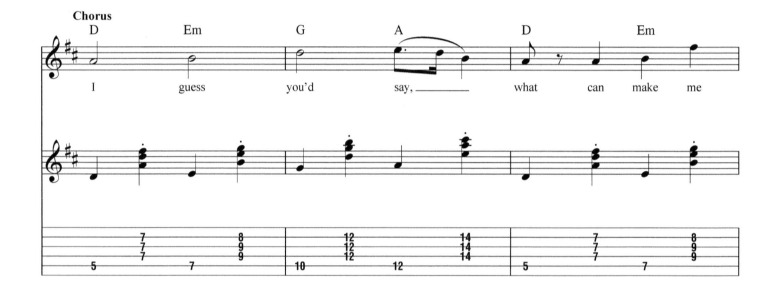

Chorus

I guess you'd say, _____ what can make me

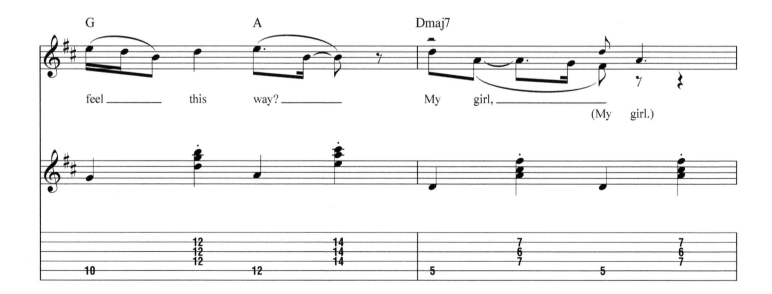

feel _____ this way? _____ My girl, _____ (My girl.)

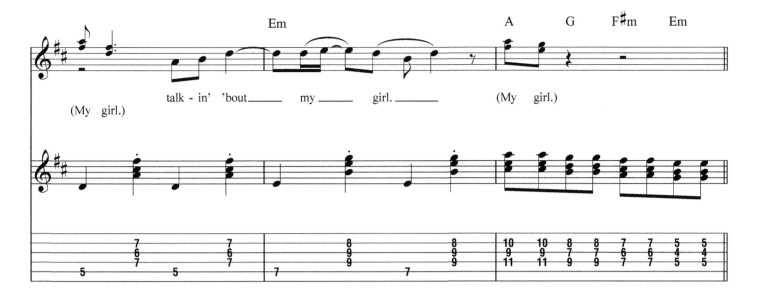

talk - in' 'bout_____ my _____ girl. _____ (My girl.)

(My girl.)

Outro
w/ Voc. ad lib., till fade
Dmaj7

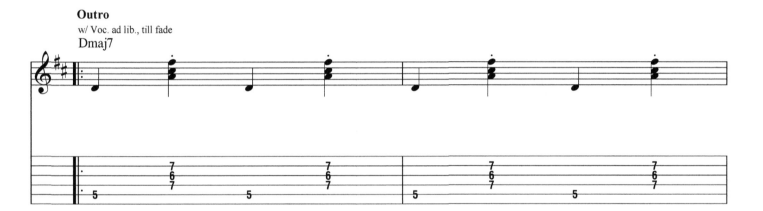

Repeat and fade

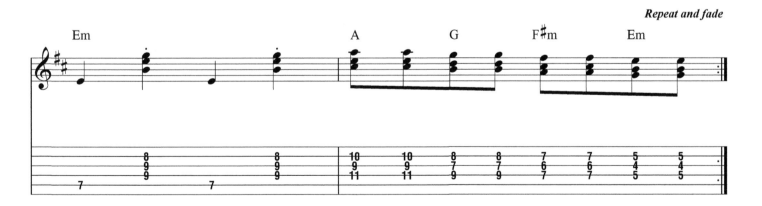

Additional Lyrics

2. I've got so much honey the bees envy me.
   I've got a sweeter song than the birds in the tree.

Shining Star

Words and Music by Maurice White, Philip Bailey and Larry Dunn

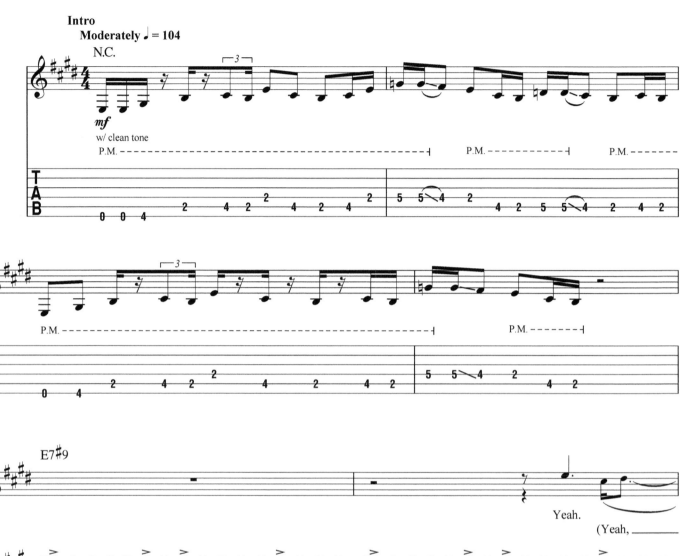

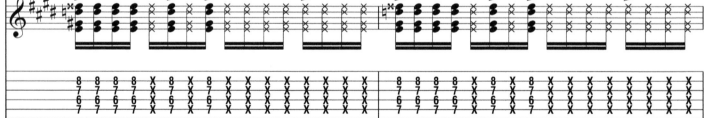

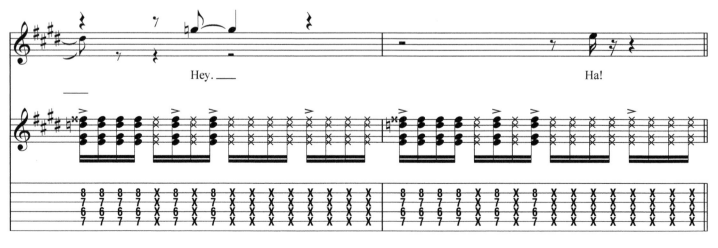

Verse

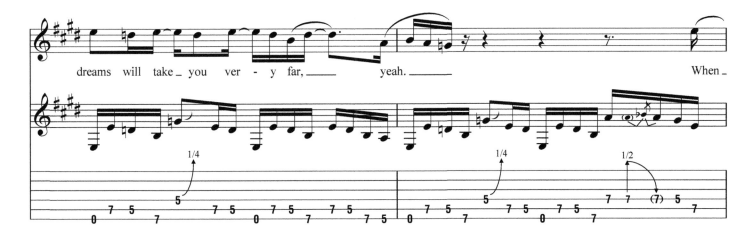

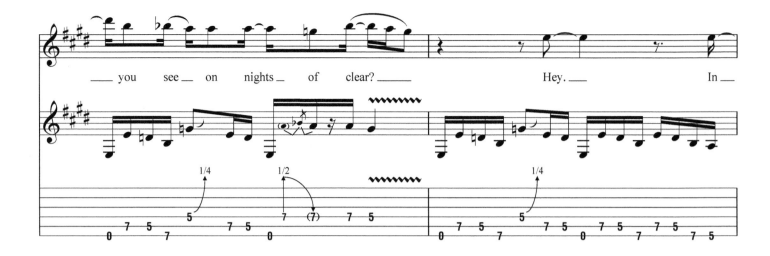

___ you see ___ on nights ___ of clear? _____ Hey. ___ In ___

___ the sky ___ so ver - y dear, ___ yeah. ___ You're a

Chorus

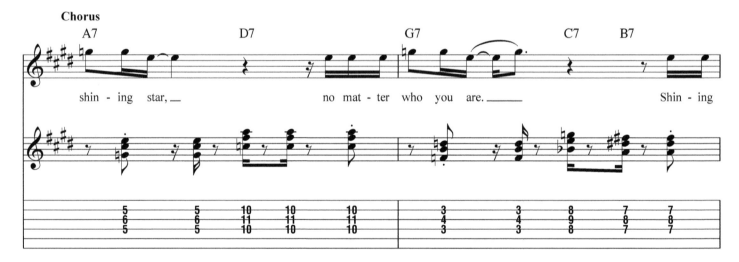

shin - ing star, ___ no mat - ter who you are. _____ Shin - ing

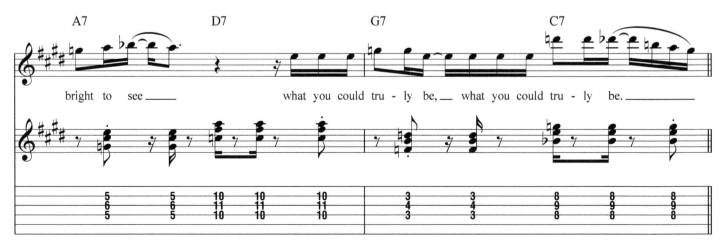

bright to see _____ what you could tru - ly be, ___ what you could tru - ly be. _____

Interlude

N.C.(Em)

Guitar Solo

N.C.(G7) (G#7) (A7)

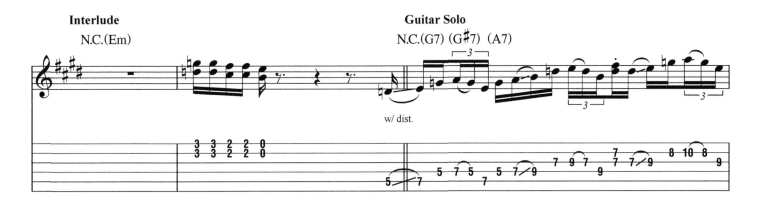

w/ dist.

(A7)　　(A#7) (B7)　　　　　　　　　(C7)　　(C#7)

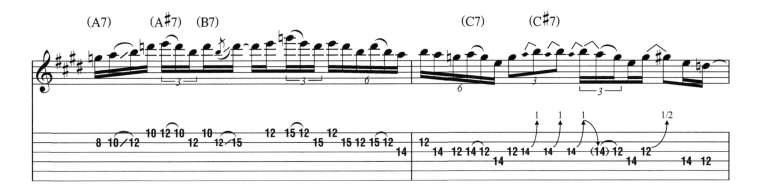

(D7)　　(D#7)　　　　　　　　　　　　　　　　(E7)

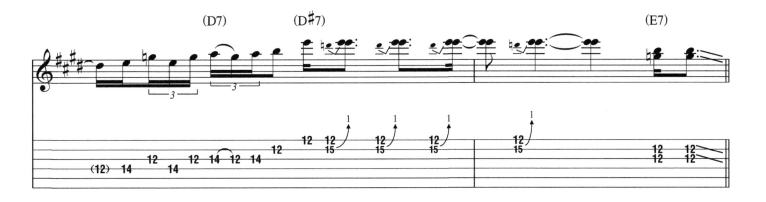

Verse

N.C.(E7#9)

2. Shin - ing　star — comes　in - to　view, —

w/ clean tone

P.M. - - - - - - - - - ┤　　　　P.M. - - - ┤

shine his watch - ful light __ on you. __ Yeah. __ Give __

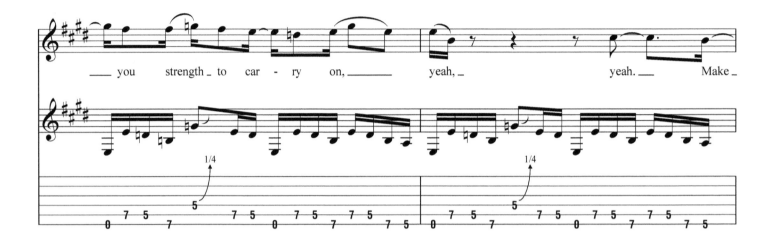

__ you strength __ to car - ry on, _____ yeah, __ yeah. __ Make __

__ your bod - y big __ and strong, _____ yeah. Born __

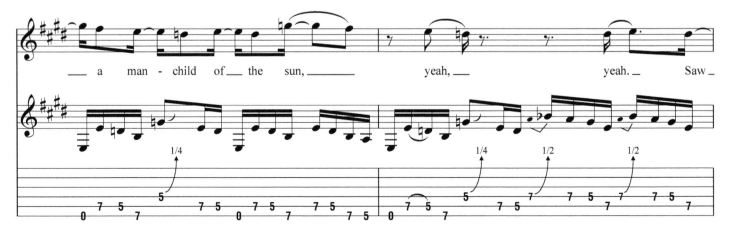

__ a man - child of __ the sun, _____ yeah, __ yeah. __ Saw __

__ my work __ had just __ be - gun. __ Yeah, __ found __

__ I had __ to stand __ a - lone, __ yeah. __ Yeah, __ bless __

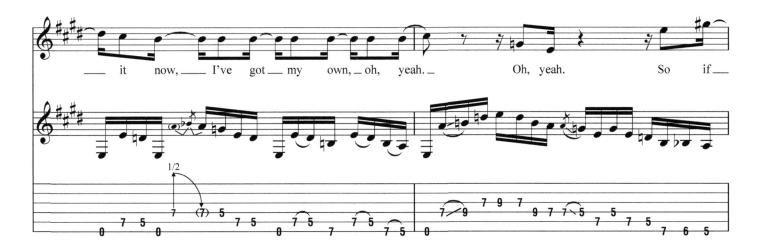

__ it now, __ I've got __ my own, _ oh, yeah. __ Oh, yeah. So if __

__ you find _ your - self __ in need, __ why _ don't you

lis - ten to ___ those words ___ of heed? ___ Be ___

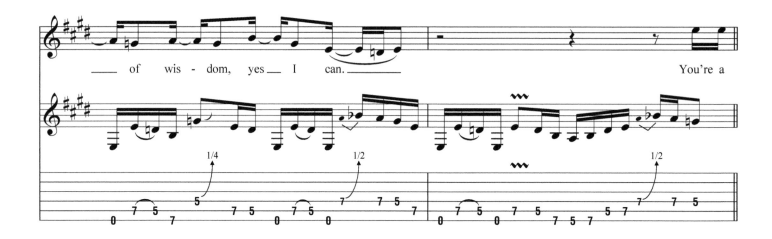

___ a gi - ant grain ___ of sand. ___ Words ___

___ of wis - dom, yes ___ I can. ___ You're a

Chorus

A7   D7   G7   C7   B7

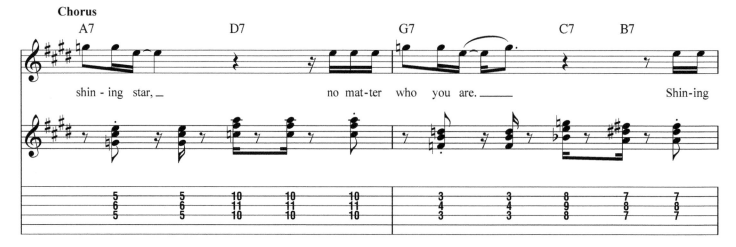

shin - ing star, ___ no mat - ter who you are. ___ Shin - ing

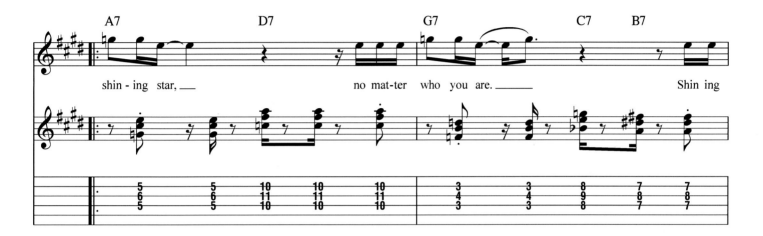

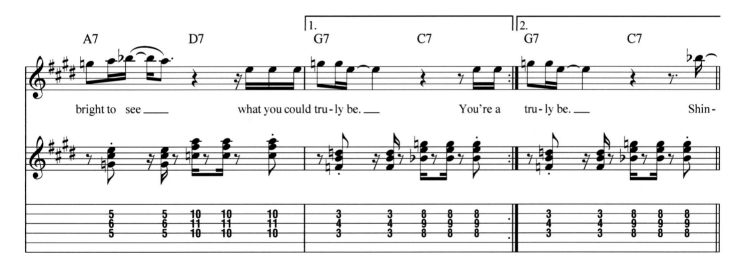

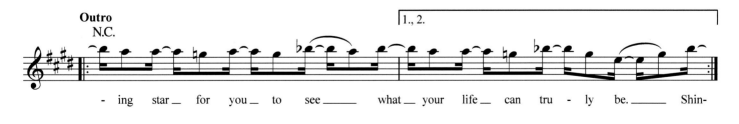

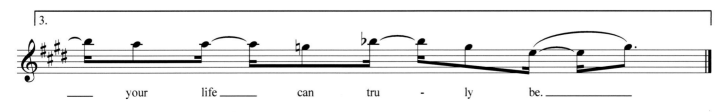

Guitar Notation Legend

THE MUSICAL STAFF shows pitches and rhythms and is divided by bar lines into measures. Pitches are named after the first seven letters of the alphabet.

TABLATURE graphically represents the guitar fingerboard. Each horizontal line represents a string, and each number represents a fret.

Notes:

Strings:

4th string, 2nd fret   1st & 2nd strings open, played together   open D chord

HALF-STEP BEND: Strike the note and bend up 1/2 step.

WHOLE-STEP BEND: Strike the note and bend up one step.

GRACE NOTE BEND: Strike the note and bend up as indicated. The first note does not take up any time.

SLIGHT (MICROTONE) BEND: Strike the note and bend up 1/4 step.

BEND AND RELEASE: Strike the note and bend up as indicated, then release back to the original note. Only the first note is struck.

PRE-BEND: Bend the note as indicated, then strike it.

VIBRATO: The string is vibrated by rapidly bending and releasing the note with the fretting hand.

PALM MUTING: The note is partially muted by the pick hand lightly touching the string(s) just before the bridge.

HAMMER-ON: Strike the first (lower) note with one finger, then sound the higher note (on the same string) with another finger by fretting it without picking.

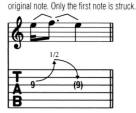

PULL-OFF: Place both fingers on the notes to be sounded. Strike the first note and without picking, pull the finger off to sound the second (lower) note.

LEGATO SLIDE: Strike the first note and then slide the same fret-hand finger up or down to the second note. The second note is not struck.

SHIFT SLIDE: Same as legato slide, except the second note is struck.

TRILL: Very rapidly alternate between the notes indicated by continuously hammering on and pulling off.

TAPPING: Hammer ("tap") the fret indicated with the pick-hand index or middle finger and pull off to the note fretted by the fret hand.

NATURAL HARMONIC: Strike the note while the fret-hand lightly touches the string directly over the fret indicated.

PINCH HARMONIC: The note is fretted normally and a harmonic is produced by adding the edge of the thumb or the tip of the index finger of the pick hand to the normal pick attack.

TREMOLO PICKING: The note is picked as rapidly and continuously as possible.

VIBRATO BAR DIVE AND RETURN: The pitch of the note or chord is dropped a specified number of steps (in rhythm) then returned to the original pitch.

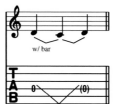

VIBRATO BAR SCOOP: Depress the bar just before striking the note, then quickly release the bar.

VIBRATO BAR DIP: Strike the note and then immediately drop a specified number of steps, then release back to the original pitch.

Additional Musical Definitions

(accent)	• Accentuate note (play it louder)	
(staccato)	• Play the note short	

D.S. al Coda • Go back to the sign (%), then play until the measure marked *"To Coda"*, then skip to the section labelled *"Coda."*

D.C. al Fine • Go back to the beginning of the song and play until the measure marked *"Fine"* (end).

Fill • Label used to identify a brief melodic figure which is to be inserted into the arrangement.

N.C. • Instrument is silent (drops out).

 • Repeat measures between signs.

1. 2. • When a repeated section has different endings, play the first ending only the first time and the second ending only the second time.

GUITAR PLAY-ALONG

INCLUDES TAB

AUDIO ACCESS INCLUDED

This series will help you play your favorite songs quickly and easily. Just follow the tab and listen to the audio to hear how the guitar should sound, and then play along using the separate backing tracks.

Playback tools are provided for slowing down the tempo without changing pitch and looping challenging parts. The melody and lyrics are included in the book so that you can sing or simply follow along.

1. ROCK
00699570.....................$17.99

2. ACOUSTIC
00699569.....................$16.99

3. HARD ROCK
00699573.....................$17.99

4. POP/ROCK
00699571.....................$16.99

5. THREE CHORD SONGS
00300985.....................$16.99

6. '90S ROCK
00298615.....................$16.99

7. BLUES
00699575.....................$19.99

8. ROCK
00699585.....................$16.99

9. EASY ACOUSTIC SONGS
00151708.....................$16.99

10. ACOUSTIC
00699586.....................$16.95

11. EARLY ROCK
00699579.....................$15.99

12. ROCK POP
00291724.....................$16.99

14. BLUES ROCK
00699582.....................$16.99

15. R&B
00699583.....................$17.99

16. JAZZ
00699584.....................$16.99

17. COUNTRY
00699588.....................$17.99

18. ACOUSTIC ROCK
00699577.....................$15.95

20. ROCKABILLY
00699580.....................$17.99

21. SANTANA
00174525.....................$17.99

22. CHRISTMAS
00699600.....................$15.99

23. SURF
00699635.....................$17.99

24. ERIC CLAPTON
00699649.....................$19.99

25. THE BEATLES
00198265.....................$19.99

26. ELVIS PRESLEY
00699643.....................$16.99

27. DAVID LEE ROTH
00699645.....................$16.95

28. GREG KOCH
00699646.....................$19.99

29. BOB SEGER
00699647.....................$16.99

30. KISS
00699644.....................$17.99

32. THE OFFSPRING
00699653.....................$14.95

33. ACOUSTIC CLASSICS
00699656.....................$19.99

34. CLASSIC ROCK
00699658.....................$17.99

35. HAIR METAL
00699660.....................$17.99

36. SOUTHERN ROCK
00699661.....................$19.99

37. ACOUSTIC UNPLUGGED
00699662.....................$22.99

38. BLUES
00699663.....................$17.99

39. '80S METAL
00699664.....................$17.99

40. INCUBUS
00699668.....................$17.95

41. ERIC CLAPTON
00699669.....................$17.99

42. COVER BAND HITS
00211597.....................$16.99

43. LYNYRD SKYNYRD
00699681.....................$22.99

44. JAZZ GREATS
00699689.....................$16.99

45. TV THEMES
00699718.....................$14.95

46. MAINSTREAM ROCK
00699722.....................$16.95

47. HENDRIX SMASH HITS
00699723.....................$19.99

48. AEROSMITH CLASSICS
00699724.....................$17.99

49. STEVIE RAY VAUGHAN
00699725.....................$17.99

50. VAN HALEN 1978-1984
00110269.....................$19.99

51. ALTERNATIVE '90S
00699727.....................$14.99

52. FUNK
00699728.....................$15.99

53. DISCO
00699729.....................$14.99

54. HEAVY METAL
00699730.....................$17.99

55. POP METAL
00699731.....................$14.95

57. GUNS N' ROSES
00159922.....................$17.99

58. BLINK-182
00699772.....................$14.95

59. CHET ATKINS
00702347.....................$17.99

60. 3 DOORS DOWN
00699774.....................$14.95

62. CHRISTMAS CAROLS
00699798.....................$12.95

63. CREEDENCE CLEARWATER REVIVAL
00699802.....................$17.99

64. OZZY OSBOURNE
00699803.....................$19.99

66. THE ROLLING STONES
00699807.....................$19.99

67. BLACK SABBATH
00699808.....................$17.99

68. PINK FLOYD – DARK SIDE OF THE MOON
00699809.....................$17.99

71. CHRISTIAN ROCK
00699824.....................$14.95

72. ACOUSTIC '90S
00699827.....................$14.95

73. BLUESY ROCK
00699829.....................$17.99

74. SIMPLE STRUMMING SONGS
00151706.....................$19.99

75. TOM PETTY
00699882.....................$19.99

76. COUNTRY HITS
00699884.....................$16.99

77. BLUEGRASS
00699910.....................$17.99

78. NIRVANA
00700132.....................$17.99

79. NEIL YOUNG
00700133.....................$24.99

81. ROCK ANTHOLOGY
00700176.....................$22.99

82. EASY ROCK SONGS
00700177.....................$17.99

84. STEELY DAN
00700200.....................$19.99

85. THE POLICE
00700269.....................$16.99

86. BOSTON
00700465.....................$19.99

87. ACOUSTIC WOMEN
00700763.....................$14.99

88. GRUNGE
00700467.....................$16.99

89. REGGAE
00700468.....................$15.99

90. CLASSICAL POP
00700469.....................$14.99

91. BLUES INSTRUMENTALS
00700505.....................$19.99

92. EARLY ROCK INSTRUMENTALS
00700506.....................$17.99

93. ROCK INSTRUMENTALS
00700507.....................$17.99

94. SLOW BLUES
00700508.....................$16.99

95. BLUES CLASSICS
00700509.....................$15.99

96. BEST COUNTRY HITS
00211615.....................$16.99

97. CHRISTMAS CLASSICS
00236542.....................$14.99

98. ROCK BAND
00700704.....................$14.95

99. ZZ TOP
00700762.....................$16.99

100. B.B. KING
00700466.....................$16.99

101. SONGS FOR BEGINNERS
00701917.....................$14.99

102. CLASSIC PUNK
00700769.....................$14.99

104. DUANE ALLMAN
00700846.....................$22.99

105. LATIN
00700939.....................$16.99

106. WEEZER
00700958.....................$17.99

107. CREAM
00701069...................................$17.99

108. THE WHO
00701053...................................$17.99

109. STEVE MILLER
00701054...................................$19.99

110. SLIDE GUITAR HITS
00701055...................................$17.99

111. JOHN MELLENCAMP
00701056...................................$14.99

112. QUEEN
00701052...................................$16.99

113. JIM CROCE
00701058...................................$19.99

114. BON JOVI
00701060...................................$17.99

115. JOHNNY CASH
00701070...................................$17.99

116. THE VENTURES
00701124...................................$17.99

117. BRAD PAISLEY
00701224...................................$16.99

118. ERIC JOHNSON
00701353...................................$17.99

119. AC/DC CLASSICS
00701356...................................$19.99

120. PROGRESSIVE ROCK
00701457...................................$14.99

121. U2
00701508...................................$17.99

122. CROSBY, STILLS & NASH
00701610...................................$16.99

123. LENNON & McCARTNEY ACOUSTIC
00701614...................................$16.99

124. SMOOTH JAZZ
00200664...................................$16.99

125. JEFF BECK
00701687...................................$19.99

126. BOB MARLEY
00701701...................................$17.99

127. 1970S ROCK
00701739...................................$17.99

128. 1960S ROCK
00701740...................................$14.99

129. MEGADETH
00701741...................................$17.99

130. IRON MAIDEN
00701742...................................$17.99

131. 1990S ROCK
00701743...................................$14.99

132. COUNTRY ROCK
00701757...................................$15.99

133. TAYLOR SWIFT
00701894...................................$16.99

135. MINOR BLUES
00151350...................................$17.99

136. GUITAR THEMES
00701922...................................$14.99

137. IRISH TUNES
00701966...................................$15.99

138. BLUEGRASS CLASSICS
00701967...................................$17.99

139. GARY MOORE
00702370...................................$17.99

140. MORE STEVIE RAY VAUGHAN
00702396...................................$19.99

141. ACOUSTIC HITS
00702401...................................$16.99

142. GEORGE HARRISON
00237697...................................$17.99

143. SLASH
00702425...................................$19.99

144. DJANGO REINHARDT
00702531...................................$17.99

145. DEF LEPPARD
00702532...................................$19.99

146. ROBERT JOHNSON
00702533...................................$16.99

147. SIMON & GARFUNKEL
14041591...................................$17.99

148. BOB DYLAN
14041592...................................$17.99

149. AC/DC HITS
14041593...................................$19.99

150. ZAKK WYLDE
02501717...................................$19.99

151. J.S. BACH
02501730...................................$16.99

152. JOE BONAMASSA
02501751...................................$24.99

153. RED HOT CHILI PEPPERS
00702990...................................$22.99

155. ERIC CLAPTON – FROM THE ALBUM UNPLUGGED
00703085...................................$17.99

156. SLAYER
00703770...................................$19.99

157. FLEETWOOD MAC
00101382...................................$17.99

159. WES MONTGOMERY
00102593...................................$22.99

160. T-BONE WALKER
00102641...................................$17.99

161. THE EAGLES – ACOUSTIC
00102659...................................$19.99

162. THE EAGLES HITS
00102667...................................$17.99

163. PANTERA
00103036...................................$19.99

164. VAN HALEN 1986-1995
00110270...................................$19.99

165. GREEN DAY
00210343...................................$17.99

166. MODERN BLUES
00700764...................................$16.99

167. DREAM THEATER
00111938...................................$24.99

168. KISS
00113421...................................$17.99

169. TAYLOR SWIFT
00115982...................................$16.99

170. THREE DAYS GRACE
00117337...................................$16.99

171. JAMES BROWN
00117420...................................$16.99

172. THE DOOBIE BROTHERS
00119670...................................$17.99

173. TRANS-SIBERIAN ORCHESTRA
00119907...................................$19.99

174. SCORPIONS
00122119...................................$19.99

175. MICHAEL SCHENKER
00122127...................................$17.99

176. BLUES BREAKERS WITH JOHN MAYALL & ERIC CLAPTON
00122132...................................$19.99

177. ALBERT KING
00123271...................................$17.99

178. JASON MRAZ
00124165...................................$17.99

179. RAMONES
00127073...................................$16.99

180. BRUNO MARS
00129706...................................$16.99

181. JACK JOHNSON
00129854...................................$16.99

182. SOUNDGARDEN
00138161...................................$17.99

183. BUDDY GUY
00138240...................................$17.99

184. KENNY WAYNE SHEPHERD
00138258...................................$17.99

185. JOE SATRIANI
00139457...................................$19.99

186. GRATEFUL DEAD
00139459...................................$17.99

187. JOHN DENVER
00140839...................................$19.99

188. MÖTLEY CRUE
00141145...................................$19.99

189. JOHN MAYER
00144350...................................$19.99

190. DEEP PURPLE
00146152...................................$19.99

191. PINK FLOYD CLASSICS
00146164...................................$17.99

192. JUDAS PRIEST
00151352...................................$19.99

193. STEVE VAI
00156028...................................$19.99

194. PEARL JAM
00157925...................................$17.99

195. METALLICA: 1983-1988
00234291...................................$22.99

196. METALLICA: 1991-2016
00234292...................................$19.99

For complete songlists, visit
Hal Leonard online at
www.halleonard.com